STEP-BY-STEP

Chinese Szechuan Cooking

STEP-BY-STEP

Chinese Szechuan Cooking

DEH–TA HSIUNG

SHOOTING STAR PRESS

This edition printed in 1995 for:
Shooting Star Press Inc
230 Fifth Avenue – Suite 1212
New York, NY 10001

Shooting Star Press books are available at special discounts for bulk purchases for sales promotions,
premiums, fund-raising, or educational use. Special edition or book excerpts can also be created to
specification. For details contact: Special Sales Director, Shooting Star Press Inc.,
230 Fifth Avenue, Suite 1212, New York, NY 10001

ISBN 1 56924 188 0

Printed in Italy

Acknowledgements:

Design & DTP: Pedro & Frances Prá-Lopez / Kingfisher Design
Art Direction: Lisa Tai
Managing Editor: Alexa Stace
Special Photography: Amanda Heywood
Home Economist: Deh-ta Hsiung
Stylist: Marian Price

Gas Hob supplied by New World Domestic Appliances Ltd
Food and equipment kindly supplied by Wing Yip
Photographs on pages 6, 18, 28, 40 & 58: By courtesy of ZEFA

Contents

CHAPTER ONE

Appetizers

Appetizers are often served as the first course or for nibbles wih
drinks in Szechuan – just like hors d'oeuvres in the West.
The advantage of these dishes is that they can generally be
prepared and even cooked well in advance – hours before serving
if need be. Also, almost all the dishes selected here are ideal
for a buffet-style meal or as party food.

Instead of serving a selection of appetizers individually, you can
serve a small portion of several or all together as an assortment.
Select a minimum of three different items such as
Deep-fried Shrimp, Bang-bang Chicken, Deep-fried Spare Ribs
and so on.

Other dishes that can be served as a part of the appetizer selection
are Szechuan Shrimp, Sweet-&-Sour Shrimp, Aromatic & Crispy
Duck, and Braised Chinese Cabbage.
Remember not to have more than one of the same type of food,
and the ingredients should be chosen for their
harmony and balance in color, aroma,
flavor and texture.

Opposite: *The Great Wall
snakes across many miles of
this vast country.*

STEP 1

STEP 2

STEP 3

STEP 4

DEEP-FRIED SHRIMP

For best results, use raw tiger shrimp in their shells. They are 3-4 in long, and you should get 18-20 shrimp per 1 lb.

SERVES 4

8-10 oz raw shrimp in their shells, defrosted
    if frozen
1 tbsp light soy sauce
1 tsp Chinese rice wine or dry sherry
2 tsp cornstarch
vegetable oil, for deep-frying
2-3 scallions, to garnish

SPICY SALT AND PEPPER:
1 tbsp salt
1 tsp ground Szechuan peppercorns
1 tsp five-spice powder

1 Pull the soft legs off the shrimp, but keep the body shell on. Dry well on paper towels.

2 Place the shrimp in a bowl with the soy sauce, wine and cornstarch. Turn to coat and leave to marinate for about 25-30 minutes.

3 To make the Spicy Salt and Pepper, mix the salt, pepper and five-spice powder together. Place in a dry skillet and stir-fry for about 3-4 minutes over a low heat, stirring constantly. Remove from the heat and allow to cool.

4 Heat the oil in a preheated wok until smoking, then deep-fry the shrimp in batches until golden brown. Remove with a slotted spoon and drain on paper towels.

5 Place the scallions in a bowl, pour on 1 tablespoon of the hot oil and leave for 30 seconds. Serve the shrimp garnished with the scallions, and with Spicy Salt and Pepper as a dip.

ROASTING SPICES

The roasted spice mixture made with Szechuan peppercorns is used throughout China as a dip for deep-fried food. The peppercorns are sometimes roasted first and then ground. Dry-frying is a way of releasing the flavors of the spices. You can make the dip in advance and store in a tightly sealed jar until ready to use.

STEP 1

STEP 2

STEP 3

STEP 4

PORK WITH CHILI & GARLIC SAUCE

Any leftovers from this dish can be used for a number of other dishes –
such as Hot-&-Sour Soup (page 20), and Twice-cooked Pork (page 53).

SERVES 4

1 lb leg of pork, boned but not skinned

SAUCE:
1 tsp finely chopped garlic
1 tsp finely chopped scallions
2 tbsp light soy sauce
1 tsp red chili oil
½ tsp sesame oil

1 Place the pork, tied together in one piece, in a large pan, add enough cold water to cover, and bring to a rolling boil over a medium heat.

2 Skim off the scum that rises to the surface, cover and simmer gently for 25-30 minutes.

3 Leave the meat in the liquid to cool, covered, for at least 1-2 hours. Lift out the meat with 2 slotted spoons and leave to cool completely, skin-side up, for 2-3 hours.

4 To serve, cut off the skin, leaving a very thin layer of fat on top like a ham. Cut the meat in small, thin slices across the grain, and arrange neatly on a plate. Mix together the sauce ingredients, then pour the sauce evenly over the pork.

SZECHUAN CHILI

One of the local Szechuan plants that contributes most to the typical character of the region's cooking is the small red *fagara* chili, which is used both fresh and dried. The chili has a delayed action on the palate; at first it seems to have little taste, but suddenly it burns the mouth with great ferocity, so it is used with much respect. It is claimed that instead of burning the taste-buds, the chili actually makes them more sensitive to other flavors.

This is a very simple dish, but beautifully presented. Make sure you slice the meat as thinly and evenly as possible to make an elegantly arranged dish.

BANG-BANG CHICKEN

The cooked chicken meat is tenderized by being beaten with a rolling pin, hence the name for this very popular Szechuan dish.

STEP 1

STEP 2

SERVES 4

4 cups water
2 chicken quarters (breast half and leg)
1 cucumber, cut into matchstick shreds

SAUCE:
2 tbsp light soy sauce
1 tsp sugar
1 tbsp finely chopped scallions
1 tsp red chili oil
¹/₄ tsp pepper
1 tsp white sesame seeds
2 tbsp peanut butter, creamed with a little
   sesame oil

4 On a flat surface, pound the chicken with a rolling pin, then tear the meat into shreds with 2 forks. Mix with the shredded cucumber and arrange in a serving dish.

5 To serve, mix together all the sauce ingredients and pour over the chicken and cucumber.

1 Bring the water to a rolling boil in a wok or a large pan. Add the chicken pieces, reduce the heat, cover and cook for 30-35 minutes.

2 Remove the chicken from the pan and immerse it in a bowl of cold water for at least 1 hour to cool it, ready for shredding.

3 Remove the chicken pieces and drain well. Dry the chicken pieces on paper towels, then take the meat off the bones.

THE CHOICEST CHICKEN

This dish is also known as Bon-bon Chicken – bon is a Chinese work for stick, so again the tenderizing technique inspires the recipe name.

Take the time to tear the chicken meat into similar-sized shreds, to make an elegant-looking dish. You can do this quite efficiently with 2 forks, although Chinese cooks would do it with their fingers.

STEP 4a

STEP 4b

STEP 1a

STEP 1b

STEP 2

STEP 3

PICKLED CUCUMBER

The pickling takes minutes rather than days – but the longer you leave it, the better the result. Some pickled vegetables are marinated for days – see the recipe for Mixed Pickled Vegetables, below.

SERVES 4

1 slender cucumber, about 12 in long
1 tsp salt
2 tsp sugar
1 tsp rice vinegar
1 tsp red chili oil
a few drops sesame oil

1 Halve the cucumber, unpeeled, lengthwise. Scrape off the seeds and cut across into thick chunks.

2 Sprinkle with the salt and mix together well. Leave to marinate for at least 20-30 minutes, longer if possible, then pour the juices away.

3 Mix the cucumber with the sugar, vinegar and chili oil, and sprinkle with the sesame oil just before serving.

MIXED PICKLED VEGETABLES

5 cups Chinese cabbage, cut into bite-sized
    pieces
2 oz French-style green beans, topped and
    tailed
1 cup carrots, diced
3 chilis, seeded and finely chopped
2 tsp Szechuan peppercorns
2 tbsp kosher salt
2 tbsp rice wine

Place the vegetables in a glass bowl with the chilies, peppercorns, salt and wine. Stir well, cover and leave to marinate in the refrigerator for 4 days. Serve cold, as a salad.

PICKLED VEGETABLES

Pickled vegetables and fruits are very popular with the Chinese. They are often served as snacks and appetizers, and can also be served with cold meat dishes. Usually the vegetables are allowed to stay in the marinade for 3-4 days. Once made, they will keep in the refrigerator for up to 2 weeks.

STEP 1

STEP 2

STEP 3

STEP 4

DEEP-FRIED SPARERIBS

*The spareribs should be chopped into small, bite-sized pieces
before or after cooking.*

SERVES 4

*8-10 finger spareribs (see box)
salt and pepper
1 tsp five-spice powder or 1 tbsp mild curry
powder
1 tbsp rice wine or dry sherry
1 egg
2 tbsp all-purpose flour
vegetable oil, for deep-frying
1 tsp finely shredded scallions
1 tsp finely shredded fresh green or red hot
chilies, seeded
Spicy Salt and Pepper (see page 8), to serve*

1 Chop the ribs into 3-4 small pieces.
Place the ribs in a bowl with salt,
pepper, five-spice or curry powder and
the wine. Turn to coat the ribs in the
spices and leave them to marinate for
1-2 hours.

2 Mix the egg and flour together to
make a batter.

3 Dip the ribs in the batter one by one
to coat well.

4 Heat the oil in a preheated wok
until smoking. Deep-fry the ribs for
4-5 minutes, then remove with a slotted
spoon and drain on paper towels.

5 Reheat the oil over a high heat and
deep-fry the ribs once more for
another minute. Remove and drain
again on paper towels.

6 Pour 1 tablespoon of the hot oil
over the scallions and chilies and
leave for 30-40 seconds. Serve the ribs
with Spicy Salt and Pepper, garnished
with the shredded scallions and chilies.

FINGER RIBS

To make finger ribs, cut the sheet of
spareribs into individual ribs down each
side of the bones. These ribs can then be
chopped into bite-sized pieces for deep-
frying.

CHAPTER TWO

Soups

Soup is not normally served as a separate course in China, except at formal occasions and banquets, when it usually appears toward the end of the meal.

Otherwise, a simply made soup is served with all the other dishes throughout a meal in Chinese homes. The soup is almost always a clear broth in which some thinly sliced vegetables and/or meat have been poached quickly.

The soup should ideally be made with a good stock. If you use a bouillon cube, remember to reduce the amount of seasoning in the recipes, since most commercially made cubes are fairly salty and spicy. It is always worthwhile making your own Chinese stock, following the recipe on page 76, if you have the time.

Opposite: *Fresh vegetables on display in a market in Szechuan. The Chinese shop daily in the markets to ensure that produce is absolutely fresh and crisp.*

STEP 1

STEP 2

STEP 3

STEP 4

HOT-&-SOUR SOUP

This is the favorite soup in Chinese restaurants throughout the world.

SERVES 4

*4-6 dried Chinese mushrooms (shiitake),
   soaked for at least 25 minutes
4 oz cooked pork or chicken
1 cake firm tofu
2 oz canned sliced bamboo shoots, drained
2½ cups Chinese Stock (see page 76) or
   water
1 tbsp Chinese rice wine or dry sherry
1 tbsp light soy sauce
2 tbsp rice vinegar
1 tbsp cornstarch paste (see page 77)
salt, to taste
½ tsp ground white pepper
2-3 scallions, thinly sliced, to serve*

1 Drain the mushrooms, squeeze dry and discard the hard stems. Thinly slice the mushrooms.

2 Thinly slice the meat, tofu and bamboo shoots into narrow shreds.

3 Bring the stock or water to a rolling boil in a wok or large saucepan and add all the ingredients. Bring back to a boil then simmer for about 1 minute. Add the wine, soy sauce and vinegar.

4 Bring back to a boil once more, stirring in the cornstarch paste to thicken the soup. Serve hot, sprinkled with the scallions.

DRIED MUSHROOMS

There are many varieties of dried mushrooms, which add a particular flavor to Chinese cooking. Shiitake mushrooms are one of the favorite kinds to use. Soak them in hot water for 25-30 minutes before use and cut off the hard stems.

If you strain the soaking liquid through fine cheesecloth, you can use the liquid to give a mushroom flavor to other soups, as well as sauces and casseroles. It is important to strain the liquid carefully because it will contain small, gritty particles.

STEP 1a

STEP 1b

STEP 2

STEP 3

THREE-FLAVOR SOUP

Ideally, use raw shrimp in this soup. If that is not possible,
add cooked ones while the soup simmers in step 3.

SERVES 4

1 cup skinned, boned chicken breast meat
4 oz raw shrimp shelled
salt
½ egg white, lightly beaten
2 tsp cornstarch paste (see page 77)
4 oz honey-roast ham
3 cups Chinese Stock (see page 76) or water
finely chopped scallions, to garnish

1 Thinly slice the chicken into small shreds. If the shrimp are large, cut each in half lengthwise, otherwise leave them whole. Place the chicken and shrimp in a bowl and mix with a pinch of salt, the egg white and cornstarch paste until well coated.

2 Cut the ham into small, thin slices roughly the same size as the chicken pieces.

3 Bring the stock or water to a rolling boil, add the chicken, the raw shrimp and the ham. Bring the soup back to a boil and simmer for 1 minute.

4 Adjust the seasoning and serve the soup hot, garnished with the scallions.

COOKING TIPS

Soups such as this are improved enormously in flavor if you use a well-flavored stock. Either use a bouillon cube, or find time to make Chinese Stock – see the recipe on page 76. Better still, make double quantities and freeze some for future use.

Fresh, uncooked shrimp impart the best flavor. If these are not available, you can use ready-cooked shrimp. They must be added at the last moment before serving to prevent them becoming tough and over-cooked.

STEP 1

STEP 2

STEP 3

STEP 4

PORK & SZECHUAN VEGETABLE

Sold in cans, Szechuan preserved vegetable is pickled mustard root.
It is quite hot and salty, so rinse it well in water before use.

SERVES 4

8 oz pork tenderloin
2 tsp cornstarch paste (see page 77)
4 oz Szechuan preserved vegetable
3 cups Chinese stock (see page 76) or water
salt and pepper
a few drops of sesame oil (optional)
2-3 scallions, sliced, to garnish

1 Cut the pork across the grain into thin shreds and mix with the cornstarch paste.

2 Wash and rinse the Szechuan preserved vegetable, then cut into thin shreds the same size as the pork.

3 Bring the stock or water to a rolling boil, add the pork and stir to separate the shreds. Return to a boil.

4 Add the Szechuan preserved vegetable and bring back to a boil once more. Adjust the seasoning and sprinkle with sesame oil. Serve hot, garnished with scallions.

SZECHUAN PRESERVED VEGETABLE

The Chinese are fond of pickles, and there are many varieties of pickled vegetables. In the Szechuan region in particular, preserved vegetables are important because the region is over 1,000 miles from the coast. Vinegar and salt (from the province's extensive salt mines) are used to make a range of pickled foods, which are used in cooking and eaten on their own.

One of the most popular is Szechuan preserved vegetable, a specialty of the province, available in cans from specialist Chinese stores or supermarkets. It is actually mustard green root, pickled in salt and chilies. It gives a crunchy, spicy taste to dishes. Rinse it in cold water before use. Once opened, the vegetable should be stored in a tightly sealed jar and kept in the refrigerator.

SPINACH & TOFU SOUP

This is a very colorful and delicious soup. If spinach is not in season, watercress or lettuce can be used instead.

STEP 1a

STEP 1b

STEP 2

STEP 3

SERVES 4

1 cake firm tofu
4 oz spinach leaves without stems
3 cups Chinese Stock (see page 76) or water
1 tbsp light soy sauce
salt and pepper

1 Cut the tofu into small pieces about ¼ in thick. Wash the spinach leaves and cut them into small pieces or shreds, discarding any discolored leaves and tough stalks. (If possible, use fresh young spinach leaves, which have not yet developed tough ribs. Otherwise, it is important to cut out all the ribs and stems for this soup).

2 In a wok or large pan, bring the stock to a rolling boil, add the tofu and soy sauce, bring back to a boil and simmer for about 2 minutes over a medium heat.

3 Add the spinach and simmer for 1 more minute.

4 Skim the surface of the soup to make it clear, adjust the seasoning and serve.

SERVING SUGGESTIONS

There is no set order of courses for Chinese meals. The soup is an integral part of the meal; it may be served first, but people can help themselves to more during the meal. The soup is usually presented in a large bowl placed in the center of the table, and consumed as the meal progresses. It serves as a refresher between different dishes and as a beverage throughout the meal. (Water is never served during the meal, and tea is brought only before and after a meal.)

Each person at the table has a bowl, rather than a plate, that is used for all dishes. Chopsticks are used for picking up the food – or in the case of soups, a broad, shallow spoon.

CHAPTER THREE

Seafood Dishes

As in the rest of China, Szechuan food features fish in many dishes, especially freshwater fish from the mighty Chang or Yangtse river, which flows through the region.

Szechuan food is noted for its hot, spicy character, and the seafood dishes are no exception. Whole fish and fish fillets are served in thick, spicy sauces, as in Braised Fish Fillets (page 37).

Shrimp dishes are equally hot and spicy, with garlic, ginger and chilies appearing in almost every recipe – Szechuan Shrimp (see page 33) is a typical example.

Opposite: The Yangtse River near Guilin. Until recently the Yangtse was Szechuan's main avenue of communication with the rest of China.

STEP 2

STEP 3a

STEP 3b

STEP 4

SWEET-&-SOUR SHRIMP

*Use raw shrimp if possible. If you are using cooked ones, however,
skip steps 1 and 2.*

SERVES 4

6-8 oz shelled raw tiger prawns or jumbo
    shrimp
pinch of salt
1 tsp egg white
1 tsp cornstarch paste (see page 77)
1¼ cups vegetable oil

SAUCE:
1 tbsp vegetable oil
½ small green bell pepper, cored, seeded and
    thinly sliced
½ small carrot, thinly sliced
1 cup canned water chestnuts, drained and
    sliced
½ tsp salt
1 tbsp light soy sauce
2 tbsp sugar
3 tbsp rice or sherry vinegar
1 tsp Chinese rice wine or dry sherry
1 tbsp tomato sauce
½ tsp chili sauce
3-4 tbsp Chinese Stock (see page 76) or
    water
2 tsp cornstarch paste (see page 77)
a few drops of sesame oil

1 Mix the shrimp with the salt, egg
white and cornstarch paste.

2 Heat the oil in a preheated wok and
stir-fry the shrimp for 30-40
seconds only. Remove and drain on
paper towels.

3 Pour off the oil and wipe the wok
clean with paper towels. To make
the sauce, first heat the tablespoon of oil.
Add the vegetables and stir-fry for about
1 minute, then add the seasonings with
the stock or water and bring to a boil.

4 Add the shrimp and stir until
blended well. Thicken the sauce
with the cornstarch paste and stir until
smooth. Sprinkle with sesame oil and
serve hot.

SESAME OIL

Sesame oil has a distinctive nutty flavor
and aroma. It is widely used in China as a
seasoning and is usually sprinkled on at
the last moment, to finish a dish. Use
sparingly. You can find it in some large
supermarkets or delicatessens or in
Chinese grocery stores.

SZECHUAN SHRIMP

Raw shrimp should be used if possible, otherwise omit steps 1 and 2 and add cooked shrimp before the sauce ingredients in step 3.

STEP 1

SERVES 4

8-10 oz raw tiger prawns or jumbo shrimp
pinch of salt
½ egg white, lightly beaten
1 tsp cornstarch paste (see page 77)
2½ cups vegetable oil
fresh cilantro leaves, to garnish

SAUCE:
1 tsp finely chopped gingerroot
2 scallions, finely chopped
1 garlic clove, finely chopped
3-4 small dried red chilies, seeded and
    chopped
1 tbsp light soy sauce
1 tsp Chinese rice wine or dry sherry
1 tbsp tomato paste
1 tbsp oyster sauce
2-3 tbsp Chinese Stock (see page 76) or
    water
a few drops of sesame oil

the shrimp in hot oil for about 1 minute. Remove with a slotted spoon and drain on paper towels.

3 Pour off the oil, leaving about 1 tablespoon in the wok. Add all the ingredients for the sauce, bring to a boil and stir until smooth and well blended.

4 Add the shrimp to the sauce and stir until blended well. Serve garnished with cilantro leaves.

STEP 2

STEP 3

1 Peel the raw shrimp, then mix with the salt, egg white and cornstarch paste until well coated.

2 Heat the oil in a preheated wok until it is smoking, then deep-fry

CHILIES

In Szechuan dishes chilies are often left unseeded, giving an extremely hot flavor. If you dislike very hot food, make sure the dried chilies are carefully seeded before use.

STEP 4

STEP 1

STEP 2

STEP 3

STEP 4

STIR-FRIED SHRIMP

The bell peppers in this dish can be replaced by either snow peas or broccoli – the idea is to contrast the pinky/orange shrimp with a bright green vegetable.

SERVES 4

6 oz raw shrimp, shelled
1 tsp salt
¼ tsp egg white
2 tsp cornstarch paste (see page 77)
1¼ cups vegetable oil
1 scallion, cut into short sections
1-in piece gingerroot, thinly sliced
1 small green bell pepper, cored, seeded and
  cubed
½ tsp sugar
1 tbsp light soy sauce
1 tsp Chinese rice wine or dry sherry
a few drops of sesame oil

1 Mix the shrimp with a pinch of the salt, the egg white and cornstarch paste until they are all well coated.

2 Heat the oil in a preheated wok and stir-fry the shrimp for 30-40 seconds only. Remove and drain on paper towels.

3 Pour off the oil, leaving about 1 tablespoon in the wok. Add the scallion and ginger to flavor the oil for a few seconds, then add the green bell pepper and stir-fry for about 1 minute.

4 Add the remaining salt and the sugar followed by the shrimp. Continue stirring for another minute or so, then add the soy sauce and wine and blend well. Sprinkle with sesame oil and serve immediately.

COOK'S HINTS

1-2 small green or red hot chilies, sliced, can be added with the green bell pepper to create a more spicy dish. Leave the chilies unseeded for a very hot dish.

Fresh gingerroot, sold by weight, should be peeled and sliced, then finely chopped or shredded before use. It will keep for weeks in a cool, dry place. Dried ginger powder is no substitute – in comparison with fresh gingerroot, it is lacking in flavor.

BRAISED FISH FILLETS

Any flat fish such as flounder or lemon sole is ideal for this dish.

STEP 2

Serves 4

3-4 small dried Chinese mushrooms
10-12 oz fish fillets
1 tsp salt
1/2 egg white, lightly beaten
1 tsp cornstarch paste (see page 77)
2 1/2 cups vegetable oil
1 tsp finely chopped gingerroot
2 scallions, finely chopped
1 garlic clove, finely chopped
1/2 small green bell pepper, cored, seeded and
    cut into small cubes
1/2 small carrot, thinly sliced
2 oz canned sliced bamboo shoots, rinsed and
    drained
1/2 tsp sugar
1 tbsp light soy sauce
1 tsp rice wine or dry sherry
1 tbsp chili bean sauce
2-3 tbsp Chinese Stock (see page 76) or
    water
a few drops of sesame oil

1 Soak the Chinese mushrooms in warm water for 30 minutes, then strain and drain on paper towels, reserving the soaking water for stock or soup. Squeeze the mushrooms to extract all the moisture, cut off and discard any hard stems and slice thinly.

2 Cut the fish into bite-sized pieces, then place in a shallow dish and mix with a pinch of salt, the egg white and cornstarch paste, turning the fish to coat well.

3 Heat the oil and deep-fry the fish pieces for about 1 minute. Remove with a slotted spoon and drain on paper towels.

4 Pour off the oil, leaving about 1 tablespoon in the wok. Add the ginger, scallions and garlic to flavor the oil for a few seconds, then add the vegetables and stir-fry for about 1 minute.

5 Add the remaining salt, sugar, soy sauce, wine, chili bean sauce and stock or water and bring to a boil. Add the fish pieces, stir to coat well with the sauce and braise for another minute. Sprinkle with sesame oil and serve immediately.

STEP 3

STEP 4

STEP 5

STEP 1

STEP 2

STEP 3a

STEP 3b

FISH IN SZECHUAN HOT SAUCE

This is a classic Szechuan recipe. When served in a restaurant, the fish head and tail are removed before cooking.

SERVES 4

1 carp, bream, sea bass, trout, grouper or
  gray mullet, about 1½ lb, drawn
1 tbsp light soy sauce
1 tbsp Chinese rice wine or dry sherry
vegetable oil, for deep-frying
flat-leaf parsley or cilantro sprigs, to garnish

SAUCE:
2 garlic cloves, finely chopped
2-3 scallions, finely chopped with the green
  and white parts separated
1 tsp finely chopped gingerroot
2 tbsp chili bean sauce
1 tbsp tomato paste
2 tsp sugar
1 tbsp rice vingar
½ cup Chinese Stock(see page 76) or water
1 tbsp cornstarch paste (see page 77)
½ tsp sesame oil

1 Wash the fish and dry well on paper towels. Score both sides of the fish to the bone with a sharp knife, making diagonal cuts at intervals of about 1 in. Rub the fish with the soy sauce and wine on both sides, then leave on a plate in the refrigerator to marinate for 10-15 minutes.

2 Heat the oil in a preheated wok until smoking. Deep-fry the fish in the hot oil for about 3-4 minutes on both sides, or until golden brown.

3 Pour off the oil, leaving about 1 tablespoon in the wok. Push the fish to one side of the wok and add the garlic, white parts of the scallions, ginger, chili bean sauce, tomato paste, sugar, vinegar and stock. Bring to a boil and braise the fish in the sauce for 4-5 minutes, turning it over once.

4 Add the green parts of the scallions and stir in the cornstarch paste to thicken the sauce. Sprinkle with sesame oil and serve immediately, garnished with parsley or cilantro.

Meat & Poultry Dishes

Poultry is popular in Szechuan as elsewhere in China, though characteristically it is much hotter and spicier than elsewhere – Szechuan Chili Chicken (page 47) is a typical example.

Beef appears on the menu more often in Szechuan than in the South or East. A favorite form of cooking is stir-frying, giving a dry, chewy texture. Braising and steaming are also popular methods of cooking beef and pork, ensuring a tender result, and so too is double-cooking. This is a technique in which the meat is first tenderized by long, slow simmering in water, followed by a quick crisping or stir-frying in a sauce – Twice-cooked Pork (page 53) is a delicious example of this technique.

Opposite: *The fertile soil of Szechuan produces abundant crops almost all the year round.*

STEP 1

STEP 2a

STEP 2b

STEP 4

AROMATIC & CRISPY DUCK

Although the pancakes traditionally served with this dish are not too difficult to make, the process is very time-consuming. Buy ready-made ones from Oriental stores, or use crisp lettuce leaves as the wrapper.

SERVES 4

2 large duckling quarters
1 tsp salt
3-4 pieces star anise
1 tsp Szechuan red peppercorns
1 tsp cloves
2 cinnamon sticks, broken into pieces
2-3 scallions, cut into short sections
4-5 small slices gingerroot
3-4 tbsp Chinese rice wine or dry sherry
vegetable oil, for deep-frying

TO SERVE:

12 ready-made thin pancakes or 12 crisp
   lettuce leaves
hoisin or plum sauce
1/4 cucumber, thinly shredded
3-4 scallions, thinly shredded

1 Rub the duckling pieces with the salt and arrange the star anise, peppercorns, cloves and cinnamon on top. Sprinkle with the scallions, ginger and wine and leave to marinate for at least 3-4 hours.

2 Arrange the duckling pieces (with the marinade spices) on a plate that will fit inside a bamboo steamer.

Pour some hot water into a wok, place the bamboo steamer in the wok, sitting on a trivet. Put in the duckling and cover with the bamboo lid. Steam the duckling pieces (with the marinade) over high heat for 2-3 hours, until tender and cooked through. Top up the hot water from time to time as required.

3 Remove the duckling and leave to cool for at least 4-5 hours – this is very important, because unless the duck is cool and dry, it will not be crispy.

4 Pour off the water and wipe the wok dry. Pour in the oil and heat until smoking. Deep-fry the duck pieces, skin-side down, for 4-5 minutes or until crisp and brown. Remove and drain on paper towels.

5 To serve, scrape the meat off the bones, place about 1 teaspoon of hoisin or plum sauce on the center of a pancake (or lettuce leaf), add a few pieces of cucumber and scallion with a portion of the duck meat. Wrap up to form a small package and eat with your fingers. Provide plenty of paper napkins for your guests.

STEP 1

STEP 2

STEP 3

STEP 4

KUNG PO CHICKEN WITH CASHEWS

Peanuts, walnuts or almonds can be used instead of the cashew nuts, if preferred.

SERVES 4

8-10 oz chicken meat, or 2 chicken breast
   halves, boned and skinned
$\frac{1}{4}$ tsp salt
$\frac{1}{3}$ egg white
1 tsp cornstarch paste (see page 77)
1 medium green bell pepper, cored and
   seeded
4 tbsp vegetable oil
1 scallion, cut into short sections
a few small slices of gingerroot
4-5 small dried red chilies, soaked, seeded
   and shredded
2 tbsp crushed yellow bean sauce
1 tsp Chinese rice wine or dry sherry
1 cup cashew nuts, roasted
a few drops of sesame oil
boiled rice, to serve

1 Cut the chicken into small cubes about the size of bouillon cubes. Place the chicken in a small bowl and mix with a pinch of salt, the egg white and the cornstarch paste, in that order.

2 Cut the green bell pepper into cubes or triangles about the same size as the chicken pieces.

3 Heat the oil in a preheated wok. Add the chicken cubes and stir-fry for about 1 minute, or until the color changes. Remove with a slotted spoon and keep warm.

4 Add the scallion, ginger, chilies and green bell pepper. Stir-fry for about 1 minute, then add the chicken with the yellow bean sauce and wine. Blend well and stir-fry for another minute. Finally stir in the cashew nuts and sesame oil. Serve hot.

VARIATIONS

Any nuts can be used in place of the cashew nuts, if preferred. The important point is the crunchy texture, which is very much a feature of Szechuan cooking.

SZECHUAN CHILI CHICKEN

In China, the chicken pieces are chopped through the bone for this dish, but if you do not own a cleaver, use filleted chicken breast meat.

STEP 1

Serves 4

1 lb chicken thighs
¹/₄ tsp pepper
1 tbsp sugar
2 tsp light soy sauce
1 tsp dark soy sauce
1 tbsp Chinese rice wine or dry sherry
2 tsp cornstarch
2-3 tbsp vegetable oil
1-2 garlic cloves, crushed
2 scallions, cut into short sections, with the
    green and white parts separated
4-6 small dried red chilies, soaked and
    seeded
2 tbsp crushed yellow bean sauce
about ²/₃ cup Chinese Stock (see page 76) or
    water

3 Add the garlic, the white parts of the scallions, the chilies and yellow bean sauce to the wok and stir-fry for about 30 seconds, blending well.

4 Return the chicken pieces to the wok, stirring constantly for about 1-2 minutes, then add the stock or water, bring to a boil and cover. Braise over medium heat for 5-6 minutes, stirring once or twice. Garnish with the green parts of the scallions and serve immediately.

STEP 2

STEP 3

1 Cut or chop the chicken thighs into bite-sized pieces and marinate with the pepper, sugar, soy sauce, wine and cornstarch for 25-30 minutes.

2 Heat the oil in a pre-heated wok, add the chicken pieces and stir-fry for about 1-2 minutes until lightly brown. Remove the chicken pieces with a slotted spoon, transfer to a warm dish and keep warm.

CHILIES

One of the striking features of Szechuan cooking is the quantity of chilies used. Food generally in this region is much hotter than elsewhere in China – people tend to keep a string of dry chilies hanging from the eaves of their houses.

STEP 4

STEP 1

STEP 2

STEP 3

STEP 4

CHICKEN WITH BELL PEPPERS

*Red bell pepper or celery can also be used in this recipe,
the method is the same.*

SERVES 4

2 chicken breast halves, boned and skinned
1 tsp salt
¹/₂ egg white
2 tsp cornstarch paste (see page 77)
1 medium green bell pepper, cored and
    seeded
1¹/₄ cups vegetable oil
1 scallion, finely shredded
a few strips of gingerroot, thinly shredded
1-2 red chilies, seeded and thinly shredded
¹/₂ tsp sugar
1 tbsp Chinese rice wine or dry sherry
a few drops of sesame oil

1 Cut the chicken breast into strips,
then mix in a bowl with a pinch of
the salt, the egg white and cornstarch, in
that order.

2 Cut the green bell pepper into thin
shreds the same size and length as
the chicken strips.

3 Heat the oil in a preheated wok,
and deep-fry the chicken strips in
batches for about 1 minute, or until the
color of the chicken changes. Remove the
chicken strips with a slotted spoon and
keep warm.

4 Pour off the excess oil from the
wok, leaving about 1 tablespoon.
Add the scallion, ginger, chilies and
green bell pepper. Stir-fry for about 1
minute, then return the chicken to the
wok together with the remaining salt,
the sugar and wine. Stir-fry for another
minute, sprinkle with sesame oil and
serve.

RICE WINE

Rice wine is used everywhere in China for
both cooking and drinking. Made from
glutinous rice, it is known as "yellow
wine" (Huang jiu or chiew in Chinese)
because of its rich amber color. The best
variety is called Shao Hsing or Shaoxing,
and comes from the south-east of China.
Rice wine is more powerful than most
wines in the West – about 16° proof – and
sherry is the best substitute as a cooking
ingredient.

STEP 1a

STEP 1b

STEP 3

STEP 4

FISH-FLAVORED SHREDDED PORK

"Fish-flavored" (yu-xiang in Chinese) is a Szechuan cooking term meaning that the dish is prepared with seasonings normally used in fish dishes.

SERVES 4

about 2 tbsp dried wood ears
8-10 oz pork tenderloin
1 tsp salt
2 tsp cornstarch paste (see page 77)
3 tbsp vegetable oil
1 garlic clove, finely chopped
1/2 tsp finely chopped gingerroot
2 scallions, finely chopped, with the white
    and green parts separated
2 celery stalks, thinly sliced
1/2 tsp sugar
1 tbsp light soy sauce
1 tbsp chili bean sauce
2 tsp rice vinegar
1 tsp Chinese rice wine or dry sherry
a few drops of sesame oil

1 Soak the wood ears in warm water for about 20 minutes, then rinse in cold water until the water is clear. Drain well, then cut into thin shreds.

2 Cut the pork into thin shreds, then mix in a bowl with a pinch of salt and about half the cornstarch paste until well coated.

3 Heat 1 tablespoon of oil in a preheated wok. Add the pork strips and stir-fry for about 1 minute, or until the color changes, then remove with a slotted spoon.

4 Add the remaining oil to the wok and heat. Add the garlic, ginger, the white parts of the scallions, the wood ears and celery. Stir-fry for about 1 minute, then return the pork strips together with the remaining salt, sugar, soy sauce, chili bean sauce, vinegar and wine. Blend well and continue stirring for another minute.

5 Finally add the green parts of the scallions and blend in the remaining cornstarch paste and sesame oil. Stir until the sauce has thickened and serve hot.

DRIED WOOD EARS

Also known as cloud ears, these are a dried gray-black fungus widely used in Szechuan cooking. They are always soaked in warm water before using. Wood ears have a crunchy texture and a mild flavor.

TWICE-COOKED PORK

Twice-cooked is a popular way of cooking meat in China. The meat is first boiled to tenderize it, then cut into strips or slices and stir-fried.

STEP 1a

STEP 1b

STEP 2

STEP 4

SERVES 4

8-10 oz shoulder or leg of pork, in one piece
4 oz canned sliced bamboo shoots, rinsed and drained
1 small green bell pepper, cored and seeded
1 small red bell pepper, cored and seeded
3 tbsp vegetable oil
1 scallion, cut into short sections
1 tsp salt
1/2 tsp sugar
1 tbsp light soy sauce
1 tsp chili bean sauce or freshly minced chili
1 tsp Chinese rice wine or dry sherry
a few drops of sesame oil

1 Immerse the pork in a pot of boiling water to cover. Return to a boil and skim the surface. Reduce the heat, cover and simmer for 15-20 minutes. Turn off the heat and leave the pork in the water to cool for at least 2-3 hours.

2 Remove the pork from the water and drain well. Trim off any excess fat, then cut into small, thin slices about the same size as the bamboo shoots. Cut the green and red bell peppers into pieces about the same size.

3 Heat the oil in a preheated wok and add the sliced vegetables together with the scallion. Stir-fry for about 1 minute.

4 Add the pork, followed by the salt, sugar, soy sauce, chili bean sauce and wine. Blend well, continue stirring for another minute, then sprinkle with sesame oil and serve.

PREPARING THE MEAT

For ease of handling, buy a boned piece of meat, and roll it into a compact shape. Tie securely with string before placing in the boiling water.

STEP 1

STEP 2

STEP 3

STEP 4

CRISPY SHREDDED BEEF

*A very popular Szechuan dish served in most Chinese restaurants
all over the world.*

SERVES 4

10-12 oz beef steak (such as sirloin)
2 eggs
¼ tsp salt
4-5 tbsp all-purpose flour
vegetable oil for deep-frying
2 medium carrots, finely shredded
2 scallions, thinly shredded
1 garlic clove, finely chopped
2-3 small fresh green or red chilies, seeded
    and thinly shredded
4 tbsp sugar
3 tbsp rice vinegar
1 tbsp light soy sauce
2-3 tbsp Chinese Stock (see page 76) or
    water
1 tsp cornstarch paste (see page 77)

1 Cut the steak across the grain into thin strips. Beat the eggs in a bowl with the salt and flour, adding a little water if necessary. Add the beef strips and mix well until coated with the batter.

2 Heat the oil in a preheated wok until smoking. Add the beef strips and deep-fry for 4-5 minutes, stirring to separate the shreds. Remove with a slotted spoon and drain on paper towels.

3 Add the carrots to the wok and deep-fry for about 1-1½ minutes, then remove with a slotted spoon and drain on paper towels.

4 Pour off the excess oil, leaving about 1 tablespoon in the wok. Add the scallions, garlic, chilies and carrots, stir-fry for about 1 minute, then add the sugar, vinegar, soy sauce and stock or water, blend well and bring to a boil.

5 Stir in the cornstarch paste and simmer for a few minutes to thicken the sauce. Return the beef to the wok and stir until the shreds of meat are well coated with the sauce. Serve hot.

TEXTURES

This dish is typical of the chewy-textured food that is so popular in Szechuan. Unlike dishes in Eastern China, many Szechuan dishes are fried with only the minimum of sauce to convey the seasonings: the sauce itself is not an important element in the dish as in Canton.

BEEF & CHILI BLACK BEAN SAUCE

It is not necessary to use the expensive cuts of beef for this recipe: the meat will be tender because it is thinly sliced and marinated.

STEP 1

SERVES 4

8-10 oz beef steak (such as sirloin)
1 small onion
1 small green bell pepper, cored and seeded
about 1¼ cups vegetable oil
1 scallion, cut into short sections
a few small slices of gingerroot
1-2 small green or red chilies, seeded and
    sliced
2 tbsp crushed black bean sauce

MARINADE:
½ tsp baking soda or baking powder
½ tsp sugar
1 tbsp light soy sauce
2 tsp Chinese rice wine or dry sherry
2 tsp cornstarch paste (see page 77)
2 tsp sesame oil

3 Heat the oil in a pre-heated wok. Add the beef strips and stir-fry for about 1 minute, or until the color changes. Remove with a slotted spoon and drain on paper towels. Keep warm.

4 Pour off the excess oil, leaving about 1 tablespoon in the wok. Add the scallion, ginger, chilies, onion and green bell pepper and stir-fry for about 1 minute. Add the black bean sauce and stir until smooth, then return the beef strips to the wok. Blend well and stir-fry for another minute. Serve hot.

STEP 2

STEP 3

1 Cut the beef into small, thin strips. Mix together the marinade ingredients in a shallow dish, add the beef strips, turn to coat and leave to marinate for at least 2-3 hours – the longer the better.

2 Cut the onion and green bell pepper into small cubes.

MARINADES

Do make sure that you marinate the beef for the time specified – it will then be wonderfully soft and tender.

STEP 4

CHAPTER FIVE

Vegetables, Rice & Noodles

With its fertile soil and warm, humid climate, Szechuan is one of
the most prosperous regions of China, and crops can be grown
almost all year round. Fruit, vegetables and cereal crops
grow in abundance, as well as mushrooms and other fungi.
Pickling, drying and salting techniques are used extensively
to help preserve this abundance of food – partly because
the humid climate makes it difficult
to keep food fresh.

As with other dishes, these tend to be highly spiced, and are usually
on the hot side. "Fish-flavored", as in the eggplant dish on page 65,
sounds strange, but is a popular way of describing dishes
cooked with a variety of spices and flavorings –
it has nothing to do with fish,
and tastes delicious!

Opposite: *Rice plants hanging
up to dry on bamboo racks. Rice
is a staple crop in China and the
fertile soil of Szechuan produces
vast quantities of it.*

STEP 1

STEP 2

STEP 3

STEP 4

MA-PO TOFU

Ma-Po was the wife of a Szechuan chef who created this popular dish in the middle of the 19th century. The beef can be replaced by Chinese dried mushrooms to make a vegetarian meal.

SERVES 4

3 cakes extra-firm or firm tofu
3 tbsp vegetable oil
4 oz coarsely ground beef
$1/2$ tsp finely chopped garlic
1 leek, cut into short sections
$1/2$ tsp salt
1 tbsp black bean sauce
1 tbsp light soy sauce
1 tsp chili bean sauce
3-4 tbsp Chinese Stock (see page 76) or
   water
2 tsp cornstarch paste (see page 77)
a few drops of sesame oil
black pepper
finely chopped scallions, to garnish

1 Cut the tofu into ½-in cubes, handling it carefully. Bring some water to a boil in a small pan or a wok, add the tofu and blanch for 2-3 minutes to harden. Remove and drain well.

2 Heat the oil in a preheated wok. Add the ground beef and garlic and stir-fry for about 1 minute, or until the color of the beef changes. Add the chopped leek, salt and sauces and blend well.

3 Add the stock or water followed by the tofu. Bring to a boil, then braise gently for 2-3 minutes.

4 Add the cornstarch paste, and stir until the sauce has thickened. Sprinkle with sesame oil and black pepper and garnish with scallions. Serve hot.

TOFU

Tofu has been an important element in Chinese cooking for more than 1,000 years. It is made of yellow soybeans, which are soaked, ground and mixed with water. Tofu is highly nutritious, being rich in protein, and has a very bland taste. Solid cakes of tofu can be cut up with a sharp knife. Cook carefully as too much stirring can cause it to disintegrate.

STEP 1a

STEP 1b

STEP 3

STEP 4

HOME-STYLE BRAISED TOFU

*The pork used in the recipe can be replaced by chicken or shrimp,
or it can be omitted altogether.*

SERVES 4

3 cakes extra firm tofu
4 oz boneless pork (or any other type
    of meat)
1 leek
1-2 scallions, cut into short sections
a few small dried whole chilies, soaked
vegetable oil, for deep-frying
2 tbsp crushed yellow bean sauce
1 tbsp light soy sauce
2 tsp Chinese rice wine or dry sherry
a few drops of sesame oil

1 Split each cake of tofu into 3 slices crosswise, then cut each slice diagonally into 2 triangles.

2 Cut the pork into small, thin slices or shreds; cut the leek into thin strips. Drain the chilies and remove the seeds using the tip of a knife, then cut into small shreds.

3 Heat the oil in a preheated wok until smoking, then deep-fry the tofu triangles for 2-3 minutes, or until golden brown all over. Remove with a slotted spoon and drain on paper towels.

4 Pour off the hot oil, leaving about 1 tablespoon in the wok. Add the pork strips, scallions and chilies and stir-fry for about 1 minute or until the pork changes color.

5 Add the leek, tofu, yellow bean sauce, soy sauce and wine and braise for 2-3 minutes, stirring very gently to blend everything well. Finally sprinkle on the sesame oil and serve.

BRAISED TOFU

Tofu is sold in 4 forms: extra firm, firm, soft or extra soft, known as silken tofu. It is the extra firm or firm kind that are used for braising and stir-frying. Silken tofu is usually added to soups, sauces, dressings or dips. It is also possible to buy dried tofu and smoked tofu in specialist Oriental stores. It is acceptable to store tofu for a few days if it is submerged in water in an air-tight container, then placed in the refrigerator.

FISH EGGPLANT

*Like Fish-flavored Shredded Pork (page 50), there is not any fish in this
dish, and the meat can be omitted without affecting the flavor.*

STEP 1

SERVES 4

1 lb eggplant
vegetable oil, for deep-frying
1 garlic clove, finely chopped
½ tsp finely chopped gingerroot
2 scallions, finely chopped, with the white
 and green parts separated
1 cup boneless pork, thinly shredded
 (optional)
1 tbsp light soy sauce
2 tsp Chinese rice wine or dry sherry
1 tbsp chili bean sauce
½ tsp salt
½ tsp sugar
1 tbsp rice vinegar
2 tsp cornstarch paste (see page 77)
a few drops of sesame oil

1 Cut the eggplant into slices and
then into thin strips about the size
of potato chips – the skin can either be
peeled or left on.

2 Heat the oil in a preheated wok
until smoking. Add the eggplant
slices and deep-fry for about 3-4 minutes,
or until soft. Remove and drain on paper
towels.

3 Pour off the hot oil, leaving about 1
tablespoon in the wok. Add the

garlic, ginger and the white parts of the
scallions, followed by the pork (if using).
Stir-fry for about 1 minute or until the
color of the meat changes, then add the
soy sauce, wine and chili bean sauce,
blending them in well.

4 Return the eggplant slices to the
wok together with the salt, sugar
and vinegar. Continue stirring for
another minute or so, then add the
cornstarch paste and stir until the sauce
has thickened.

5 Add the green parts of the scallions
to the wok and sprinkle on the
sesame oil. Serve hot.

STEP 2

STEP 3

FISH-FLAVORED
DISHES

These multiple-flavored dishes, using
garlic, chili sauce, vinegar, sugar and soy
sauce all together, are always described
as "fish-flavored", although there is not
any fish in the recipe. These dishes are
only found in Szechuan.

STEP 4

STEP 1

STEP 2

STEP 3

STEP 4

STIR-FRIED SEASONAL VEGETABLES

When selecting different fresh vegetables for this dish, bear in mind that there should always be a contrast in color as well as texture.

SERVES 4

1 medium red bell pepper, cored and seeded
4 oz zucchini
4 oz cauliflower
4 oz French-style green beans
3 tbsp vegetable oil
a few small slices gingerroot
$^{1}/_{2}$ tsp salt
$^{1}/_{2}$ tsp sugar
Chinese Stock (see page 76) or water
1 tbsp light soy sauce
a few drops of sesame oil (optional)

1 Cut the red bell pepper into small squares. Thinly slice the zucchini. Trim the cauliflower and divide into small flowerets, discarding any thick stems. Make sure the vegetables are cut into roughly similar shapes and sizes to ensure even cooking.

2 Top and tail the green beans, then cut them in half.

3 Heat the oil in a preheated wok, add the vegetables and stir-fry with the ginger for about 2 minutes.

4 Add the salt and sugar to the wok, and continue to stir-fry for 1-2 minutes, adding a little Chinese stock

or water if the vegetables appear to be too dry. Do not add liquid unless it seems necessary.

5 Add the light soy sauce and sesame oil (if using) blend well to lightly coat the vegetables and serve immediately.

VEGETABLES

Almost any vegetables can be used in this dish: other good choices would be snow peas, broccoli flowerets, carrots, baby corn cobs, green peas, Chinese cabbage and young spinach leaves. Either white or black (oyster) mushrooms can also be used to give a greater diversity of textures. Make sure there is a good variety of color, and always include several crisp vegetables such as carrots or snow peas.

66

STEP 1

STEP 2

STEP 3

STEP 4

BRAISED CHINESE CABBAGE

White cabbage can be used instead of the Chinese variety for this dish.

SERVES 4

1 lb Chinese cabbage or white cabbage
3 tbsp vegetable oil
½ tsp Szechuan red peppercorns
5-6 small dried red chilies, seeded and
*   chopped*
½ tsp salt
1 tbsp sugar
1 tbsp light soy sauce
1 tbsp rice vinegar
a few drops of sesame oil (optional)

1 Shred the Chinese cabbage or cabbage crosswise into thin pieces. (If Chinese cabbage is unavailable, the best alternative to use in this recipe is a firm-packed white cabbage, not the dark green type of cabbage. Cut out the thick core of the cabbage with a sharp knife before shredding.)

2 Heat the oil in a pre-heated wok, add the Szechuan red peppercorns and dried red chilies and stir for a few seconds.

3 Add the Chinese cabbage or shredded cabbage to the peppercorns and chilies, stir-fry for about 1 minute, then add salt and continue stirring for another minute.

4 Add the sugar, soy sauce and vinegar, blend well and braise for 1 more minute. Finally sprinkle on the sesame oil, if using. Serve hot or cold.

PEPPERCORNS

It is important to use the correct type of peppercorns in preparing this dish. Szechuan red peppercorns are also known as farchiew. They are not true peppers, but reddish brown dry berries with a pungent, aromatic odor which distinguishes them from the hotter black peppercorns. Roast them briefly in the oven or sauté them in a dry skillet. Grind the peppercorns in a blender and store in a jar until needed.

STEP 1

STEP 2

STEP 3

STEP 4

CHICKEN OR PORK CHOW MEIN

This is a basic recipe – the meat and/or vegetables can be varied as much as you like.

SERVES 4

8 oz Chinese egg noodles
4-5 tbsp vegetable oil
4 oz French-style green beans
8 oz chicken breast meat, or pork fillet,
   cooked
2 tbsp light soy sauce
1 tsp salt
1/2 tsp sugar
1 tbsp Chinese rice wine or dry sherry
2 scallions, finely shredded
a few drops of sesame oil
chili sauce, to serve (optional)

1 Cook the noodles in boiling water according to the directions on the package, then drain and rinse under cold water. Drain again, then toss with 1 tablespoon of the oil.

2 Slice the meat into thin shreds and top and tail the beans.

3 Heat 3 tablespoons of oil in a preheated wok until hot, add the noodles and stir-fry for 2-3 minutes with 1 tablespoon soy sauce, then remove to a serving dish. Keep warm.

4 Heat the remaining oil and stir-fry the beans and meat for about 2 minutes. Add the salt, sugar, wine, the remaining soy sauce and about half the scallions to the wok.

5 Blend the meat mixture well and add a little stock if necessary, then pour on top of the noodles and sprinkle with sesame oil and the remaining scallions. Serve hot or cold with or without chili sauce.

CHOW MEIN

Chow Mein literally means "stir-fried noodles" and is highly popular in the West, as well as in China. Almost any ingredient can be added, such as fish, meat, poultry or vegetables. It is very popular for lunch and makes a tasty salad served cold.

70

STEP 2

STEP 3

STEP 4

STEP 5

NOODLES IN SOUP

*Noodles in soup (tang mein) are far more popular than fried noodles
(chow mein) in China. You can use different ingredients
for the dressing according to taste.*

SERVES 4

8 oz chicken fillet, pork tenderloin, or any
    other boneless cooked meat
3-4 Chinese dried mushrooms, soaked for at
    least 25 minutes
4 oz canned sliced bamboo shoots, rinsed and
    drained
1¹/₂ cups spinach leaves, lettuce hearts or
    Chinese cabbage
2 scallions, finely shredded
8 oz Chinese egg noodles
2¹/₂ cups Chinese Stock (see page 76)
2 tbsp light soy sauce
2 tbsp vegetable oil
1 tsp salt
¹/₂ tsp sugar
2 tsp Chinese rice wine or dry sherry
a few drops of sesame oil
1 tsp red chili oil (optional)

1 Cut the meat into thin shreds.
Squeeze dry the soaked
mushrooms and discard the hard stems.

2 Thinly shred the mushrooms,
bamboo shoots and scallions.

3 Cook the noodles in boiling water
according to the directions on the
package, then drain and rinse under cold

water. Place in a bowl. Bring the stock to
a boil, add about 1 tablespoon soy sauce
and pour over the noodles. Keep warm.

4 Heat the oil in a preheated wok,
add about half of the scallions, the
meat and the vegetables (mushrooms,
bamboo shoots and greens). Stir-fry for
about 2-3 minutes. Add all the
seasonings and blend well.

5 Pour the mixture in the wok over
the noodles, garnish with the
remaining scallions and serve
immediately.

NOODLE SOUP

Noodle soup is wonderfully satisfying and
is ideal to serve on cold winter days.

EGG FRIED RICE

The rice used for frying should not be too soft. Ideally, the rice should have been slightly under-cooked and left to cool before frying.

STEP 1

SERVES 4

3 eggs
1 tsp salt
2 scallions, finely chopped
2-3 tbsp vegetable oil
3 cups cooked rice, well drained and cooled
  (see note in step 3)
1 cup cooked peas

1 Lightly beat the eggs with a pinch of salt and 1 tablespoon of the scallions.

2 Heat the oil in a preheated wok, add the eggs and stir until lightly scrambled. (The eggs should only be cooked until they start to set, so they are still moist.)

3 Add the rice and stir to make sure that each grain of rice is separated. Note: the cooked rice should be cool, preferably cold, so that much of the moisture has evaporated. This ensures that the oil will coat the grains of rice and prevent them sticking. Store the cooked rice in the refrigerator until ready to cook. Make sure the oil is really hot before adding the rice, to avoid the rice being saturated with oil otherwise it will be heavy and greasy.

4 Add the remaining salt, scallions and peas. Blend well and serve hot or cold.

STEP 2

PERFECT FRIED RICE

Use rice with a fairly firm texture. Ideally, the raw rice should be soaked in water for a short time before cooking. The two main varieties of rice available are long-grain and short-grain. While it used to be necessary to wash rice, processing now makes this unnecessary. Short-grain Oriental rice can be substituted for long-grain.

Fried rice lends itself to many variations. You may choose to add other vegetables as well as the scallions, if desired, as well as shrimp, ham or chicken.

STEP 3

STEP 4

SZECHUAN COOKING

CHINESE STOCK

This basic stock is used not only as the basis for soup-making, but also for general use in Chinese cooking.

MAKES 2½ QUARTS

1½ lb chicken pieces
1½ lb pork spareribs
3¾ quarts cold water
3-4 pieces gingerroot, crushed
3-4 scallions, each tied into a
knot
3-4 tbsp Chinese rice wine or dry
sherry

1. Trim off excess fat from the chicken and spareribs; chop them into large pieces.

2. Place the chicken and pork in a large pan with water. Add the ginger and scallion knots.

3. Bring to a boil, then skim off the scum. Reduce the heat and simmer, uncovered, for at least 2-3 hours.

4. Strain the stock, discarding the chicken, pork, ginger and scallions. Add the wine and return to a boil, then simmer for 2-3 minutes.

Refrigerate the stock when cool; it will keep up to 4-5 days. Alternatively, it can be frozen in small containers and be defrosted as required.

Szechuan, the largest single province in China, lies in a great basin ringed with mountains. Its principal connection eastward is through spectacular gorges cut by the Chang or Yangtse river – until recently, in fact, the Yangtse was its only means of communication with the outside world. With its fertile soil and warm, humid climate, crops can be grown almost all the year round, and it has always been one of the most prosperous regions of China. Fruit and vegetables grow in abundance, as well as edible mushrooms and other fungi. Spices grow in abundance here, too, particularly chilies and the famous Szechuan peppercorns.

Szechuan food is noted for being hot, spicy and strongly flavored. Chilies are used in large quantities – usually unseeded – as well as pungent-flavored vegetables such as garlic, onions and scallions. The inhabitants also enjoy the aromatic, nutty flavor of peanuts, sesame seeds, cashews, walnuts and pine nuts, which are often found incorporated into dishes; aromatic ground rice and sesame seeds are often used to coat meat which is to be deep-fried or stir-fried, while sesame paste is often the principal ingredient in sauces.

The region is also noted for its food preservation techniques, which include salting, drying, smoking and pickling, probably because the humid climate makes it difficult to keep food fresh.

Beef appears more often on the menu here than in the south. A favorite way of cooking it is by stir-frying, often until it is quite dry, giving it the characteristic dry, "chewy" texture. Steaming is also popular, and here the meat is usually first coated with ground rice, producing a rich, thick gravy.

Yunnan, in the deep southwest, is even more remote than Szechuan. Being so mountainous and secluded, it developed over the years a highly distinctive cuisine of its own. The best known product of Yunnan is its ham, which many Chinese consider the best in the world. It is also noted for its game, such as rabbit and venison, and it is here that such exotic items as bear's paws, snails, armadillo, slugs and snakes can appear on the menu!

EQUIPMENT AND UTENSILS

There are only a few basic implements in the Chinese *batterie de cuisine* that are considered essential to achieve the best results. Equivalent equipment is always available in a Western kitchen, but Chinese cooking utensils are of an ancient design, usually made of inexpensive materials; they have been in continuous use for several thousand of years and do serve a special function. Their more sophisticated and much more expensive Western counterparts prove rather inadequate in contrast.

Chinese cleaver An all-purpose cook's knife that is used for slicing, shredding, peeling, crushing and chopping. Different sizes and weights are available.

Wok The round-bottomed iron wok conducts and retains heat evenly, and because of its shape, the ingredients always return to the center, where the heat is most intense, however vigorously you stir. The wok is also ideal for deep-frying – its conical shape requires far less oil than the flat-bottomed deep-fat fryer, and has more depth (which means more heat) and more cooking surface (which means more food can be cooked at one go). Besides being a skillet, a wok is also used for braising, steaming, boiling and poaching – in other words, the whole spectrum of Chinese cooking methods can be executed in one single utensil.

Ladle and spatula Some wok sets come with a pair of stirrers in the form of a ladle and spatula. Of the two, the flat ladle or scooper (as it is sometimes called) is more versatile. It is used by the Chinese cook for adding ingredients and seasonings to the wok besides being a stirring implement.

Strainers There are two basic types of strainers – one is made of copper or steel wire with long bamboo handles, the other of perforated metal (iron or stainless steel). Several different sizes are available.

Steamers The traditional Chinese steamer is made of bamboo and they can be stacked on top of each other. The modern version is made of aluminum. Of course, the wok can be used on its own as a steamer with a rack or trivet and the dome-shaped wok lid.

Chopsticks Does Chinese food taste any better when eaten with chopsticks? This is not merely an aesthetic question, but also a practical point, partly because all Chinese food is prepared in such a way that it is easily picked up by chopsticks.

Learning to use chopsticks is quite simple and easy – place one chopstick in the hollow between thumb and index finger and rest its lower end below the first joint of the third finger. This chopstick remains stationary. Hold the other chopstick between the tips of the index and middle finger, steady its upper half against the base of the index finger, and use the tip of the thumb to keep it in place. To pick up food, move the upper chopstick with index and middle fingers.

GLOSSARY OF INGREDIENTS USED IN CHINESE COOKING

Baby corn Baby corn cobs have a wonderfully sweet fragrance and flavor, and an irresistible texture. They are available both fresh and in jars.

Bamboo shoots Available in cans only. Once opened, the contents may be kept in fresh water in a covered jar for up to a week in the refrigerator.

Bean sprouts Fresh bean sprouts, from mung or soybeans, are widely available from Oriental stores and supermarkets. They can be kept in the refrigerator for two to three days.

Black bean sauce Sold in jars or cans. Salted beans are crushed and mixed with flour and spices (such as ginger, garlic or chilies) to make a thick paste.

CORNSTARCH PASTE

Cornstarch paste is made by mixing 1 part cornstarch with about 1½ parts of cold water. Stir until smooth. The paste is used to thicken sauces.

SHRIMP WITH DIP SAUCE

10 oz raw shrimp, defrosted if frozen
1 tsp salt
4 cups water
2 scallions, shredded
2-3 slices gingerroot, shredded
2 green or red chilies, seeded and finely shredded
1 tbsp vegetable oil
2 tbsp light soy sauce
1 tbsp red rice vinegar
1 tsp sesame oil

1. Poach the shrimp in boiling, salted water for 1 minute, then turn off the heat. Leave to stand for 1 minute then remove with a slotted spoon and drain.

2. Place the scallions, ginger and chilies in a small heatproof bowl. Heat the oil until hot and pour into the bowl. Add the soy sauce, vinegar and sesame oil.

3. Shell the shrimp, leaving the tails, and arrange on a serving dish. Serve with the dip sauce.

PLAIN RICE

Use long-grain or patna rice, or better still, try fragrant Thai rice.

SERVES 4
1 1/4 cups long-grain rice
about 3/4 cup cold water
pinch of salt
1/2 tsp oil (optional)

1. Rinse the rice just once. Place the rice in a saucepan and add enough water so that there is no more than ¾ in of water above the surface of the rice.

2. Bring to a boil, then add salt and oil (if using) and stir to prevent the rice from sticking to the bottom of the pan.

3. Reduce the heat to very, very low, cover and cook for 15-20 minutes.

4. Remove from the heat and let stand, covered, for 10 minutes or so. Fluff up the rice with a fork or spoon before serving.

Once opened, keep in the refrigerator.

Chili bean sauce Fermented bean paste mixed with hot chilies and other seasonings. Sold in jars, some sauces are quite mild, but others are very hot. You will have to try out the various brands to see which one is to your taste.

Chili sauce Very hot sauce made from chilies, vinegar, sugar and salt. Usually sold in bottles and should be used sparingly in cooking or as a dip. Hot-pepper sauce can be a substitute.

Chinese cabbage Also known as bok choy, there are two widely available varieties in supermarkets and greengrocers. The most commonly seen one is a pale green color and has a tightly wrapped, elongated head – about two-thirds of the cabbage is stem, which has a crunchy texture. The other variety has a shorter, fatter head with curlier, pale yellow or green leaves, also with white stems.

Cilantro Fresh cilantro leaves, also known as Chinese parsley or coriander, are widely used in Chinese cooking as a garnish.

Dried Chinese mushrooms (shiitake) Highly fragrant dried mushrooms which add a special flavor to Chinese dishes. There are many different varieties, but shiitake are the best. They are not cheap, but a small amount will go a long way, and they will keep indefinitely in an airtight jar. Soak them in warm water for 20-30 minutes (or in

cold water for several hours), squeeze dry and discard the hard stems before use.

Egg noodles There are many varieties of noodles in China, ranging from flat, broad ribbons to long narrow strands. Both dried and fresh egg noodles are available.

Five-spice powder A mixture of star anise, fennel seeds, cloves, cinnamon bark and Szechuan pepper. It is very pungent, so should be used sparingly. It will keep in an airtight container indefinitely.

Gingerroot Fresh gingerroot, sold by weight, should be peeled and then sliced, finely chopped or shredded before use. It will keep for weeks in a dry, cool place. Dried ginger powder is no substitute.

Hoisin sauce This is made from soybeans, sugar, flour, vinegar, salt, garlic, chilies and sesame seed oil. Sold in cans or jars, it will keep in the refrigerator for several months.

Oyster sauce A thick soy-based sauce used as a flavoring in Cantonese cooking. Sold in bottles, it will keep in the refrigerator for months.

Plum sauce Plum sauce has a unique, fruity flavor – a sweet-and-sour sauce with a difference.

Rice vinegar There are two basic types of rice vinegar. Red vinegar is made from fermented rice and has a distinctive dark color and depth of flavor. White vinegar is stronger in flavor because it is distilled from rice wine.

Rice wine Chinese rice wine, made from glutinous rice, is also known as "yellow wine" (Huang jiu or chiew in Chinese), because of its golden amber color. The best variety is called Shao Hsing or Shaoxing from southeast China. A good dry or medium sherry can be an acceptable substitute.

Sesame oil This aromatic oil is sold in bottles and widely used as a finishing touch, added to dishes just before serving. The refined yellow sesame oil sold in middle-eastern stores is not so aromatic, has less flavor and therefore is not a very satisfactory substitute for the real thing.

Soy sauce Sold in bottles or cans, this popular Chinese sauce is used both for cooking and at the table. Light soy sauce has more flavor than the sweeter, dark soy sauce, which gives the food a rich, reddish color.

Straw mushrooms Grown on beds of rice straw, hence the name, straw mushrooms have a pleasant slippery texture, and a subtle taste. Canned straw mushrooms should be rinsed and drained after opening.

Szechuan peppercorns Also known as farchiew, these are wild reddish-brown peppercorns from Szechuan. More aromatic but less hot than either white or black peppercorns, they do give a quite

unique flavor to the food.

Szechuan preserved vegetable The pickled mustard root is very hot and salty. Sold in cans. Once opened, it should be stored in a tightly sealed jar in the refrigerator.

Tofu (bean curd) This custard-like preparation of puréed and pressed soybeans is exceptionally high in protein. It is usually sold in cakes about 3 in square and 1 in thick in Oriental and health-food stores. It will keep for a few days if submerged in water in a container and placed in the refrigerator.

Water chestnuts The roots of the plant *Heleocharis tuberosa*. Also known as horse's hooves in China on account of their appearance before the skin is peeled off. They are available fresh or in cans. Canned water chestnuts do not have the texture, and even less the flavor, of fresh ones. Will keep for about a month in the refrigerator in a covered jar, changing the water every two or three days.

Wood ears Also known as cloud ears, this is a dried black fungus. Sold in plastic bags in Oriental stores, it should be soaked in cold or warm water for 20 minutes, then rinsed in fresh water before use. It has a crunchy texture and a mild but subtle flavor.

Yellow bean sauce A thick paste made from salted, fermented yellow soybeans, crushed with flour and sugar. It is sold in cans or jars.

CHINESE FRUIT SALAD

The Chinese do not usually have desserts to finish off a meal, except at banquets and special occasions. Sweet dishes are usually served in between main meals as snacks, but fruit is refreshing at the end of a big meal.

8 oz rock candy or crystal sugar
2½ cups boiling water
1 large honeydew melon
4-5 different fruits, such as pineapple, grapes, banana, mango, lychees or kiwi fruit

1. Dissolve the rock candy in the boiling water, then leave to cool.

2. Slice 1 in off the top of the melon and scoop out the flesh, discarding the seeds. Cut the flesh into small chunks. Prepare the other fruits and cut into small chunks.

3. Fill the melon shell with the fruits and the syrup. Cover with plastic wrap and chill for at least 2 hours. Serve on a bed of crushed ice.

INDEX